KT-210-399

Scouts in Bondage

*And Other Curious Works from
Bygone Times with Titles that
Might Cause Vulgar Minds
to Misapprehend
their Content*

Compiled by Mr MICHAEL BELL
Bookseller of Lewes,
East Sussex

Aurum Press

Based on the original limited edition
Telling Titles, compiled by Michael Bell
and designed by Ornan Rotem

First published 2006 by Aurum Press Ltd,
25 Bedford Avenue, London WC1B 3AT

Selection and design copyright © 2006 by Michael Bell

All rights reserved. No part of this book may be
reproduced or utilised in any form or by any means,
electronic or mechanical, including photocopying,
recording or by any information storage and retrieval
system, without permission in writing from Aurum
Press Ltd.

A catalogue record for this book is available
from the British Library

ISBN-10 1 84513 196 7
ISBN-13 978 1 84513 196 8

6   5   4   3   2
2011   2010   2009   2008   2007   2006

Layout and photography: Ornan Rotem

Printed in Slovenia by MKT Print d. d.

Preface

ITS OWN SMALL WAY, this little volume sets out to alleviate a local traffic hazard. On the narrows of my local High Street in Lewes, pedestrian progress has been regularly impeded over the last few years by gatherings of idlers stalled before the window of the Caburn Bookshop. Turning their backs on the striding shoppers, the revving vehicles and the town's Tourist Information Centre, these people, with apparently nothing better to do, stand giggling and nudging elbows at the bibliographical oddments displayed there by the proprietor, Mr Michael Bell. Now, the publication of the cream of his 'NOT FOR SALE' display makes it possible for them to relocate these essentially anti-social activities to the privacy of their own homes.

It is one thing to promote a taste for the past through heritage packaging, as in the Information Centre's window. It is quite another, across the street, to be catching out bygone Britain with its cultural pants down. Surely, it's rather shameful? Consider how the face of Wilhelmina Stitch must have lighted up at that moment when the resolution formed in her mind: I will write a book; it shall be called Homespun! Think with what dedication, with what private intensities of imaginative effort she laboured long hours to foist upon the world this unlooked for boon. The tremulous pride with which she yielded her parcel of longhand to the post office clerk; the assiduous exchanges between Methuen & Co., their copy-editors, illustrators and printers, full of little thoughtfulnesses ('An inset picture on the spine might add to the volume's appeal'); the anxious wait to publication day; the solitary, disappointingly noncommittal review in the *Leicester Evening Post* of 18 February 1930 … . How can you bear to sustain that heartless smirk?

Easily. To find things funny is to get them into focus. Hindsight gives a surer perspective on what's past than 'heritage' presentation. Modestly, this volume offers glimpses of a vast, unmappable hinterland of preposterous aspirations, stretching over one hundred and twenty years of publishing, expressed in mad and exquisite niceties of typography, iconography and diction. Anyone's aspirations, not only those of Wilhelmina Stitch (and of those who christened her), are liable to turn ludicrous. Soon, too, this innocent artefact will be found irredeemably guilty, caught out bang to rights in the crime of being past its sell-by date.

Julian Bell

The Books

Amy Grey

Willie's Ordeal

The Religious Tract Society, London
UNDATED [c. 1924]

4½" × 7½"

" Here's the money if you like to part with the rabbit"
57

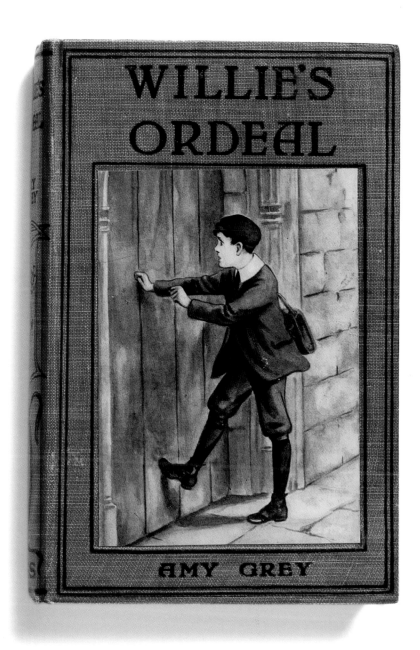

WILLIE'S ORDEAL

AMY GREY

'Maria Monk'

Awful Disclosures of Maria Monk

What I have written is true!

Modern Fiction (London) Ltd
UNDATED

4½" × 7"

The events, places and persons mentioned in this novel
are entirely fictitious and are not to be confused
with any actual events and persons, living or dead.

AWFUL DISCLOSURES OF

MARIA MONK

What I have written is true!

H.W.PERL

Dr E. Muir

How to Recognise Leprosy
A Popular Guide

Publisher not stated
UNDATED

7" × 10"

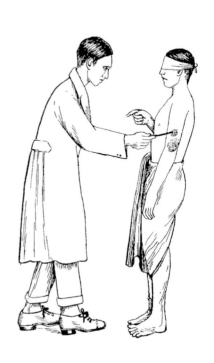

HOW TO RECOGNISE LEPROSY

A POPULAR GUIDE

BY

Dr. E. MUIR.

[Author not credited]

*Book of Blank Maps
with Instructions*

W. Foulsham & Co., Limited, London
UNDATED

5½" × 9"

BOOK of
BLANK MAPS

WITH INSTRUCTIONS

LONDON :

W. FOULSHAM & CO., LIMITED

PRICE ONE SHILLING AND SIXPENCE NET

Frank Topham

Invisible Dick

D. C. Thomson & Co. Ltd, London
1931

5¼" × 8¼"

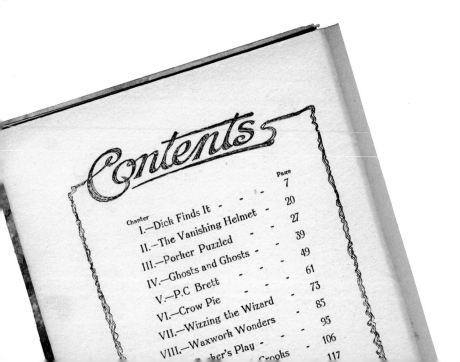

Contents

INVISIBLE
DICK

by
Frank
Topham

Miss H. H. Tuxford, M. C. A

Cookery For The Middle Classes

With Special Chapter on Vegetarian Cookery
Useful Hints on Gas Stove Cooking

Abel Heywood & Son, Manchester

UNDATED

4½" × 7"

SHEEP'S HEAD BROTH.

1 sheep's head, 3 or 4 Brussels sprouts, 1 turnip, 2ozs. pearl barley, 2 quarts cold water, 1 carrot, 1 onion, 1 dessert spoonful parsley, pepper and salt.

METHOD.—Wash head well and remove slimy part, also soft part of nostrils. Put in pan with water and barley, allow to boil, and remove scum. Add carrot, turnip, and onion, which should be cut into small pieces, and simmer four hours. About 20 minutes before dishing add shredded Brussels sprouts or cabbage leaf shredded. Take out the head and serve broth with chopped parsley on top.

The meat of the head can be chopped finely and mixed with pepper, salt, butter, and powdered sage, and put into meat pots, if liked.

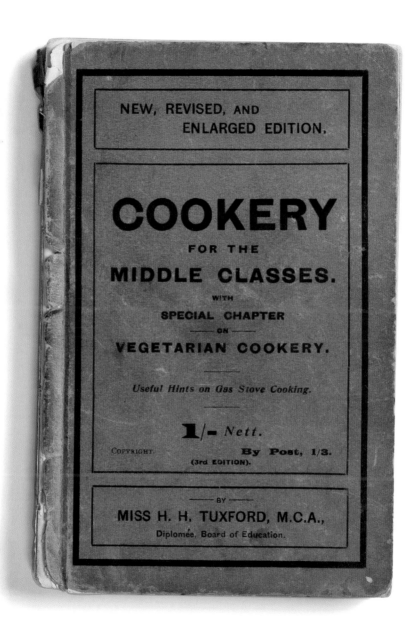

NEW, REVISED, AND
ENLARGED EDITION.

COOKERY

FOR THE
MIDDLE CLASSES.

WITH

SPECIAL CHAPTER

ON

VEGETARIAN COOKERY.

Useful Hints on Gas Stove Cooking.

1/- *Nett.*

COPYRIGHT. **By Post, 1/3.**
(3rd EDITION).

BY

MISS H. H. TUXFORD, M.C.A.,

Diplomée, Board of Education.

Frances E. Willard

With an introduction by Sir Benjamin Ward Richardson

A Wheel Within A Wheel

How I Learned to Ride the Bicycle
with some Reflections by the Way

Hutchinson & Co., London

1895

4¼" × 6¾"

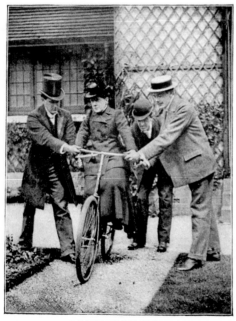

A LACK OF BALANCE.

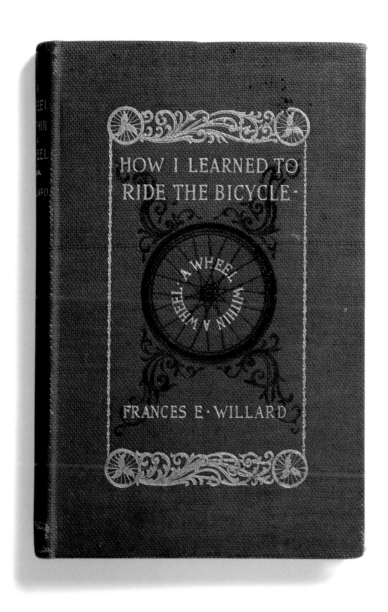

HOW I LEARNED TO
RIDE THE BICYCLE·

A WHEEL
WITHIN A WHEEL

FRANCES E·WILLARD

[Author not credited]

Girls' Interests

The Vereston Annuals

D. L. M. S., London
UNDATED [c. 1937]

7¾" × 11"

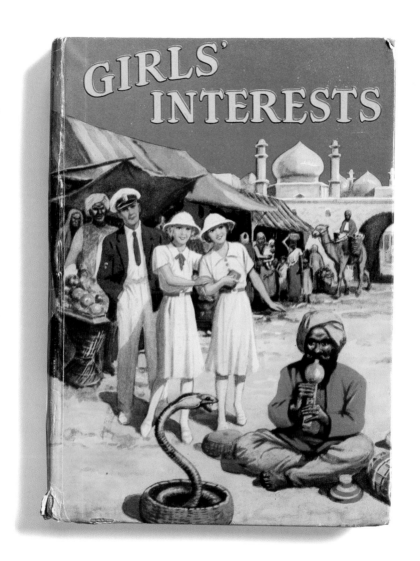

GIRLS' INTERESTS

'Julian'
Illustrated by John R. Biggs

50 Faggots

John Miles Publisher Ltd, London
UNDATED

5" × 7½"

50

FAGGOTS

by

JULIAN

Illustrated by JOHN R. BIGGS

JOHN MILES

Hans Müller-Casenov
Illustrations by C. E. Brock

The Humour of Germany
With Introduction and Biographical Index

Walter Scott Ltd, London
1892

5½" × 7½"

"SEVEN ELONGATED FACES HERE STARTED UP."

INTERNATIONAL
HUMOUR

THE HUMOUR
OF
GERMANY

Edward M. Chrystie

Leathers in Mozambique

An Adventure Story for Boys

Hodder and Stoughton, London

1959

5¼" × 7½"

Leathers in Mozambique

EDWARD M. CHRYSTIE

Mrs Bagot Stack

Building the Body Beautiful
The Bagot Stack Stretch-and-swing System

Chapman and Hall Limited, London
1931

7½" × 9½"

BUILDING THE BODY BEAUTIFUL

THE BAGOT STACK STRETCH-AND-SWING SYSTEM

By
MRS. BAGOT STACK

LONDON
CHAPMAN AND HALL LIMITED
11, HENRIETTA STREET, W.C. 2
1931

Bessie Marchant

How Nell Scored

Thomas Nelson and Sons Ltd, London
UNDATED

5" × 7¼"

Bertram Smith

Totty
The Truth about Ten Mysterious Terms

Latimer House Limited, London
1950

$7\frac{1}{2}'' \times 9\frac{1}{2}''$

TOTTY

The Truth about
Ten Mysterious Terms

by

Bertram
Smith

Stephen J. Williams

Welsh in a Week

A Rapid Method of Learning Welsh
by means of Conversation

Evans & Short, Tonypandy
UNDATED

5" × 7"

K. Akadaa & J. Satomi

How to Speak
Japanese Correctly

Okazakiya Shoten, Tokyo
1930

3" × 6"

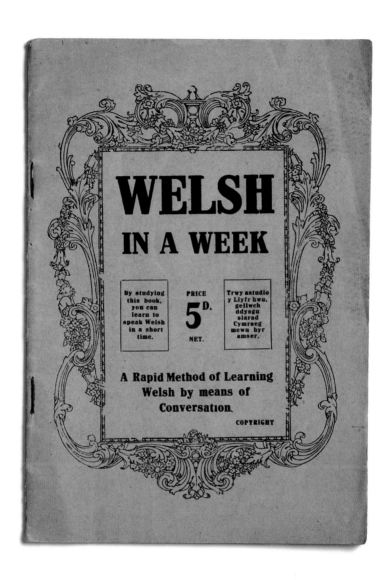

WELSH
IN A WEEK

By studying this book, you can learn to speak Welsh in a short time.

PRICE
5D.
NET.

Trwy astudio y Llyfr hwn, gellwch ddysgu siarad Cymraeg mewn byr amser,

A Rapid Method of Learning Welsh by means of Conversation.

COPYRIGHT

Mrs O. F. Walton

Christie's Old Organ
or *'Home Sweet Home'*

The Religious Tract Society, London
UNDATED [c. 1888]

4¾" × 7"

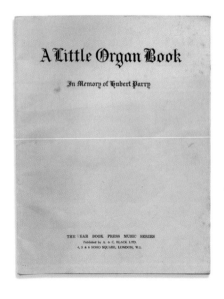

[Author not credited]

*A Little
Organ Book*

A. & C. Black, London
UNDATED

8½" × 11"

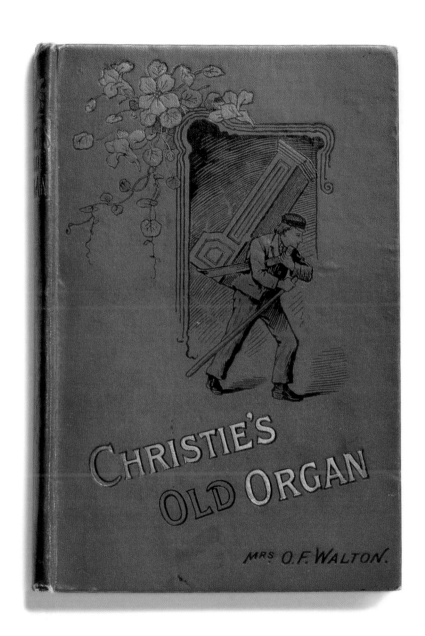

CHRISTIE'S
OLD ORGAN

MRS O. F. WALTON.

Introduction by Juan Ainaud de Lasarte
Photographs by Fazio

Tossa

Aymá, Barcelona
1957

6½" × 8"

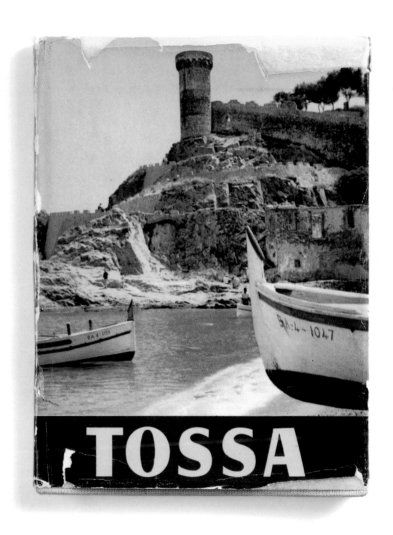

TOSSA

Pearl Binder

Muffs and Morals

George G. Harrap & Co. Ltd, London
1953

8" × 5½"

FASHION IN BEARDS, 1855

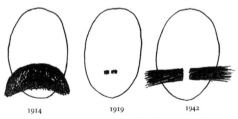

1914   1919   1942

MILITARY MOUSTACHES OF THE TWENTIETH CENTURY

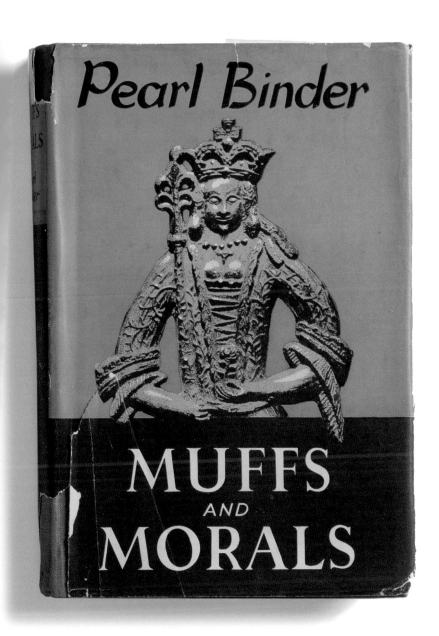

Pearl Binder

MUFFS
AND
MORALS

[Author not credited]

What To Do If It's Catching

Newron, Chambers & Co. Limited, nr Sheffield
UNDATED

$5\frac{1}{4}" \times 8\frac{1}{4}"$

When nursing sick children, never
kiss anyone on the mouth.

WHAT TO DO
if it's
CATCHING

1/-

C. T. Reeves

The Day Amanda Came

Victory Press (Evangelical Publishers Ltd),
London and Eastbourne
1971

5" × 7½"

Desmond Reid

The Corpse Came Too!

Sexton Blake Library, London
1961

5¼" × 7"

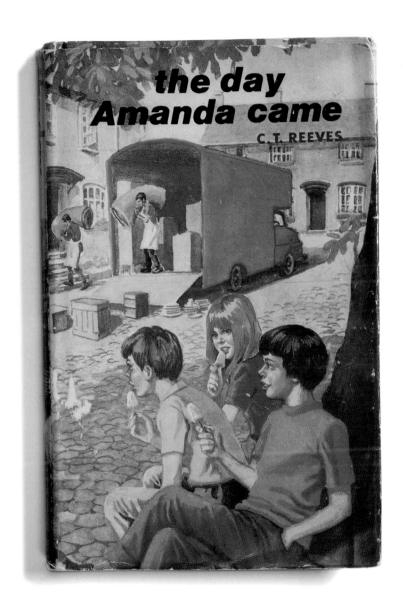

the day
Amanda came

C. T. REEVES

Geoffrey Prout
Author of *Trawler Boy Dick* etc.

Scouts in Bondage
A Story of Boy Scouts in Strange Adventure

The Goodship House, London
UNDATED

$6" \times 7\frac{1}{2}"$

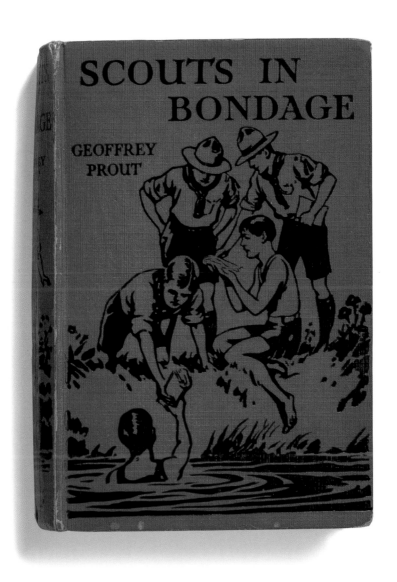

SCOUTS IN BONDAGE

GEOFFREY PROUT

G. Lister Sutcliffe, A.R.I.B.A, M.R.S.I., (editor)

The Modern Plumber and Sanitary Engineer

Treating of Plumbing, Sanitary Works, Ventilation,
Heating (Electric and other), Hot-water Services,
Gas-fitting, Electric Lighting, Bell-
work, Glazing, &c.

The Gresham Publishing Company Ltd, London

UNDATED

6¾" × 10"

Where made bends are fixed, it is usual to fit connectors or running sockets to them (fig. 81). The barrel is screwed with an equal thread for a distance of 3 in.; on this is run a back-nut, or, as some term it, a jam-nut, the outer face of which is turned out hollow. A socket is also threaded on to the screwed pipe. The pipe is butted against the screw of the next length, the joint painted and packed, the socket run up tight on the short screw, and a grummet of twisted hemp soaked in red-lead is put behind the socket on the screwed pipe; the back-nut is screwed up hard against the socket, squeezing the grummet between. This is a joint that can easily be undone when any repairs or alterations are required. Plumbers, when fitting up iron pipes for any purpose, should never fail to fix connectors at many points, as means of access to the pipe systems.

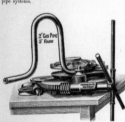

Fig. 80.—Kennedy's Patent Pipe-bending Machine

Fig 81.—Connector for Wrought-iron Pipe

Expansion and Contraction.—In fixing long lengths of hot-water pipes, allowance must be made for the expansion and contraction of the pipe during the varying heat. This can be done by making an **S** or **U** bend on one length, which will receive the thrust of the expanding pipe, and recoil as it cools.

Fixing Wrought-iron Pipes.—Wrought-iron pipes are sometimes fixed with pipe- and wall-hooks, the pipe lying hard against the wall. It is best to use proper pipe-hooks or suspenders; these are built into the wall, and have a ring in two halves (fig. 77), of the same size as the pipe, which stands an inch clear of the wall. The pipe is laid in the bottom half of the clip, and the other half is added and screwed up tight. By this means the pipe is kept off the wall, and is easily accessible for repairs.

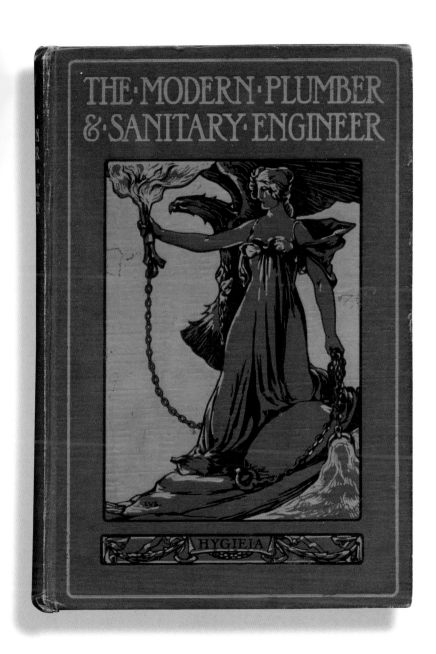

THE·MODERN·PLUMBER
&·SANITARY·ENGINEER

HYGIEIA

James Laver, editor
Illustrated by Walter Goetz

Memorable Balls

Derek Verschoyle, London
1954

8½" × 11"

MEMORABLE BALLS

Edited by James Laver

Illustrated by Walter Goetz

London
DEREK VERSCHOYLE

Wilhelmina Stitch
Author of *The Fragrant Minute for Every Day*

Homespun

Methuen & Co. Ltd, London
1930

4" × 6¾"

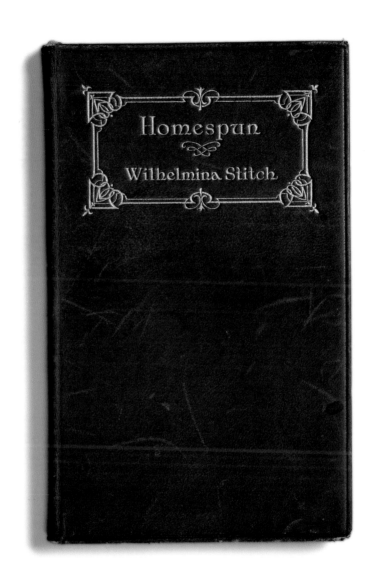

Homespun

Wilhelmina Stitch

H. Courtney Bryson

Rock Climbs Round London

*Being a guide with which are incorporated some refined
Decorations in exquisite taste by Edmund Dulac as
well as an introduction by Geoffrey Winthrop
Young and a preface with useful hints.*

ALL VERY PROPER
*to be read and kept in
the best families.*

Printed for H. Courtney Bryson
at St. George's Press, Brentford
1936

5" × 7"

ROCK CLIMBS ROUND LONDON
H. COURTNEY BRYSON

Mrs Rodolph Stawell
Illustrated in colour by Edmund Dulac

Fairies I Have Met

John Lane, The Bodley Head, London
1907

6" × 8"

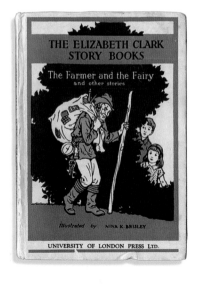

Elizabeth Clark
Illustrated by Nina K. Brisley

*The Farmer
and the Fairy*

University of
London Press, London
1936

4¾" × 6¾"

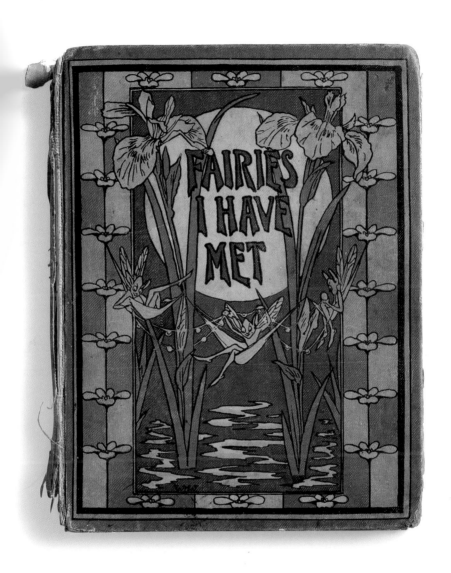

Lillie B. & Arthur C. Horth

101 Things for Girls To Do

*Being a Review of Simple Crafts
and Household Subjects*

B. T. Batsford Ltd, London

1935

5" × 7½"

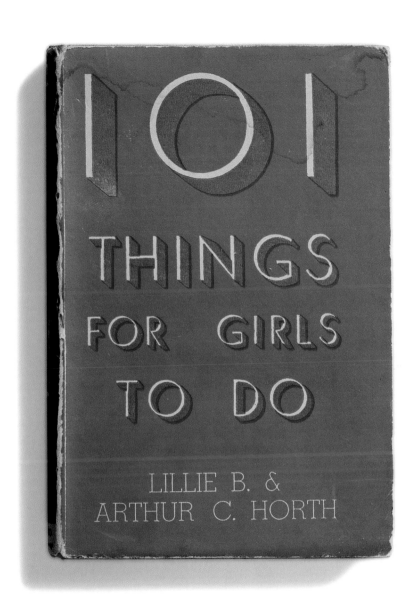

101
THINGS
FOR GIRLS
TO DO

LILLIE B. &
ARTHUR C. HORTH

George Gentry

Hardening and Tempering Engineers' Tools

Model & Allied Publications, Hemel Hempstead

1971

5" × 7½"

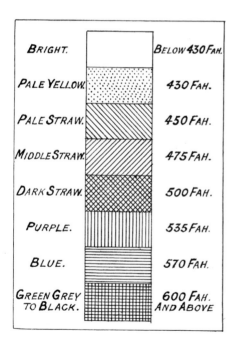

Hardening
and
Tempering
ENGINEERS' TOOLS

MAP TECHNICAL PUBLICATION 50p

Compiled by H. Childs, F. R. HIST. S.

Self-Education for the Police

Police Review Publishing Co. Ltd, London

UNDATED

4" × 6½"

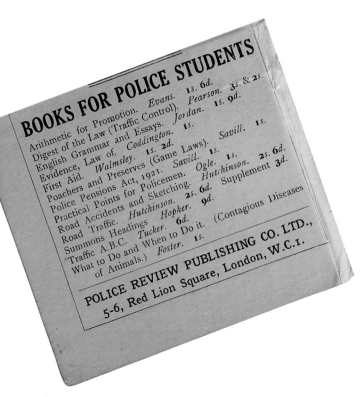

BOOKS FOR POLICE STUDENTS

Arithmetic for Promotion. *Evans.* 1s. 6d.
Digest of the Law (Traffic Control). *Pearson.* 3s. & 2s.
English Grammar and Essays. *Jordan.* 1s. 9d.
Evidence, Law of. *Coddington.* 1s.
First Aid. *Walmsley.* 1s. 2d.
Poachers and Preserves (Game Laws). *Savill.* 1s.
Police Pensions Act, 1921. *Savill.* 1s.
Practical Points for Policemen. *Ogle.* 1s.
Road Accidents and Sketching. *Hutchinson.* 2s. 6d.
Road Traffic. *Hutchinson.* 2s. 6d. Supplement 3d.
Summons Headings *Hopker.* 9d.
Traffic A.B.C. *Tucker.* 6d. (Contagious Diseases
What to Do and When to Do it. *Foster.* 1s.
of Animals.)

POLICE REVIEW PUBLISHING CO. LTD.,
5-6, Red Lion Square, London, W.C.I.

SELF-EDUCATION
FOR THE
POLICE

Evelyn Everett Green

"Let's Toss for It"
or, The Gambler's Career

James B. Knapp, London
1891

5" × 6¾"

Lydia Hoyt Farmer

The World's Famous Queens

Walter Scott Limited, London
UNDATED

6" × 8"

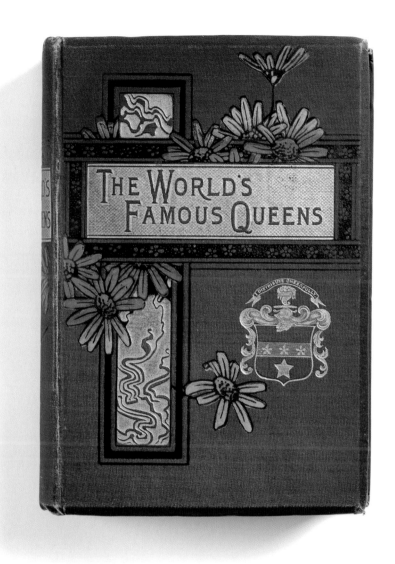

THE WORLD'S
FAMOUS QUEENS

Francis B. Cooke

Single-Handed Cruising

Edward Arnold & Co., London
1931

5½" × 9"

Charles Sutton

The Danger of Cruising
and other Poems

Sherratt & Hughes, Manchester
1937

6" × 7"

SINGLE·HANDED·
·CRUISING·

The Danger of Cruising
and other Poems

By
CHARLES SUTTON

[Author not credited]

The Girl Guide Knot Book

Brown, Son & Ferguson Ltd, Glasgow
1933

$4\frac{3}{4}" \times 7"$

Fig. 123.

THE
GIRL GUIDE
KNOT BOOK

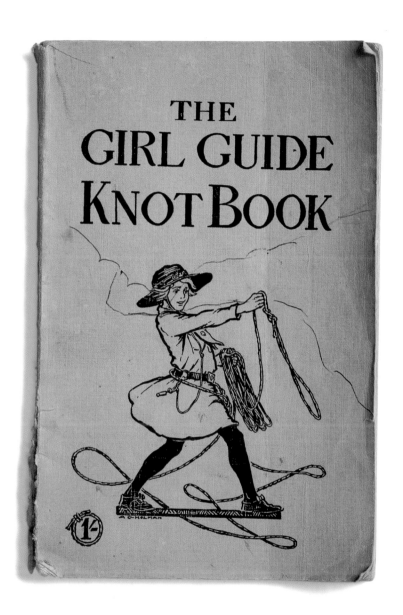

A.C.HOLMAN

1/-

Russell V. Allin, M. INST. C. E.

The Resistance of
Piles to Penetration

Tables of Approximate Values
Based on the Hiley Formula

E. & F. N. Spon Ltd, London

1935

5" × 9"

THE
RESISTANCE OF PILES
TO PENETRATION

RUSSELL V. ALLIN

'Tom Tit'
(translated & adapted by
Professor Cargill G. Knott)

Scientific Amusements

Thomas Nelson & Sons, London
UNDATED [c. 1920]

6¾" × 9½"

Scientific Amusements

by Tom Tit

Clare Goslett

Simple Hints for Mothers on the
Home Sex-training of Boys
Little Boyhood

Mrs. Clare Goslett, Ealing

UNDATED

4" × 6¼"

SOME DANGERS.

From some influences and experiences, which must always be immoral and dangerous, the mother should protect her little boy as far as possible. Spectacles of pain and sights of cruelty are debasing to the whole nature. We have abundant proofs of this where children in certain classes of life are allowed to go to slaughter-houses, or are taken to see 'the kill' of the stag in hunting districts, a sight considered lucky by the parents.

It is not good for one child to see another receive corporal punishment.

Exciting plays and cinematograph shows, especially those in which murder scenes or acts of cruelty are represented, may act as an unwholesome stimulus to immature sex functions. Stories that depict extravagant love scenes, displays of

30

SIMPLE HINTS FOR MOTHERS

ON THE

HOME SEX-TRAINING OF BOYS.

LITTLE BOYHOOD.

— BY —

CLARE GOSLETT.

4

Price Threepence,

By Post, Fourpence.

To be obtained of—

Mrs. CLARE GOSLETT, Kenilworth, Craven Avenue, Ealing, W

James C. Thomson
Illustrations by C. Leslie Thomson, B. SC.

Two Health Problems
Constipation and Our Civilisation

The connection between our Indigestion
and our Indecision; Our Food and
Our Behaviour. Advertising
Specialists, Pain, Drugs
and Enemas...

With suggestions for Home Treatment.

Thorsons Publishers Ltd, London
1954

5¼" × 7½"

TWO HEALTH PROBLEMS

CONSTIPATION
and
OUR CIVILISATION

By

JAMES C. THOMSON

Of the KINGSTON CLINIC, EDINBURGH

The connection between our Indigestion
and our Indecision; Our Food and
Our Behaviour.   Advertising Specialists,
Pain, Drugs and Enemas .   .   .
With suggestions for Home Treatment.

Illustrations by
C. LESLIE THOMSON, B.Sc.

MONOGRAPH

THORSONS PUBLISHERS LTD.
91 St. Martin's Lane, London, W.C.2

Harold Avery

A Toast Fag

Thomas Nelson and Sons, London
UNDATED

5" × 7½"

A TOAST
FAG

'M. B.'

Autobiography of
the Best Abused Man in the World

Griffith, Farran and Co., London
UNDATED

4½" × 7"

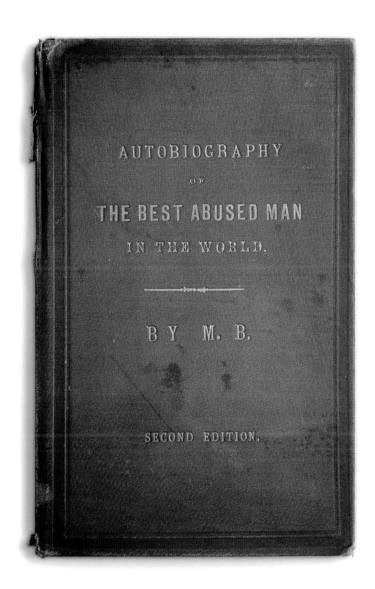

AUTOBIOGRAPHY

OF

THE BEST ABUSED MAN

IN THE WORLD.

BY M. B.

SECOND EDITION.

Florence B. Jack, editor

The Woman's Book

Contains Everything a Woman Ought to Know

T. C. & E. C. Jack, Edinburgh

1911

7" × 9¼"

FIG. 1. FIG. 2. FIG. 3. FIG. 4. FIG. 5.

FIG. 6. 7. FIG. 8. FIG. 9. FIG. 10.

THE
WOMAN'S
BOOK
·
CONTAINS
EVERYTHING
A·WOMAN
OUGHT
TO·KNOW

M. B. Manwell

The Captain's Bunk
A Story for Boys

The Religious Tract Society, London
UNDATED

5" × 7"

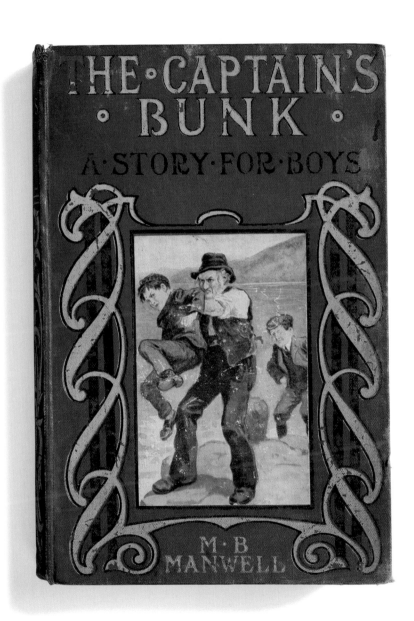

THE·CAPTAIN'S
·BUNK·

A·STORY·FOR·BOYS

M·B
MANWELL

Charles Fearnley

Health and Handlebars

Including the Author's 'Handlebar Course of Exercises'
and an additional chapter by Reg. Harris.
Fully Illustrated.

Published by the Author, London

1949

5" × 7"

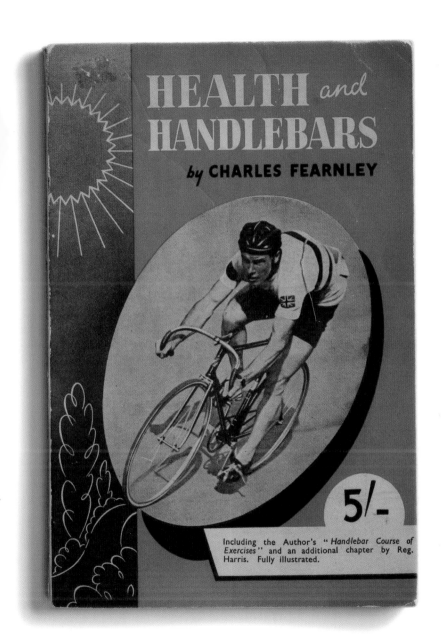

HEALTH *and* HANDLEBARS

by CHARLES FEARNLEY

5/-

Including the Author's "*Handlebar Course of Exercises*" and an additional chapter by Reg. Harris. Fully illustrated.

Agnes & Egerton Castle

Pamela Pounce

A Tale of Tempestuous Petticoats

Hodder and Stoughton Ltd, London
UNDATED

$5" \times 7\frac{1}{2}"$

PAMELA POUNCE
A TALE OF
TEMPESTUOUS PETTICOATS
·
AGNES & EGERTON CASTLE

Capt. W. G. Hartog, A. E. C. , M. A. B. LITT.,
Officier d'Academie

French for the Troops

Send this to your Soldier friend,
You'll be helping Him

Collins, London and Glasgow
1941

4½" × 7"

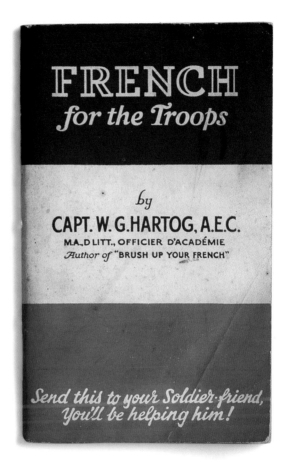

FRENCH
for the Troops

by

CAPT. W. G. HARTOG, A.E.C.

M.A., D LITT., OFFICIER D'ACADÉMIE

Author of "BRUSH UP YOUR FRENCH"

Send this to your Soldier-friend,
You'll be helping him!

[Author not credited]

Incurables & Humour

Publisher not stated
1920

6" × 9"

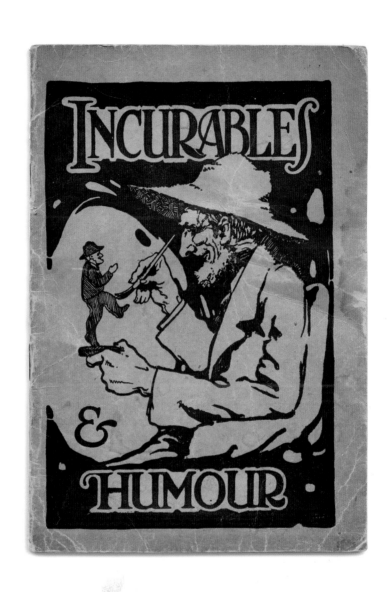

Paolo Mantegazza

The Art of Taking a Wife

Gay and Bird, London
1894

5" × 8"

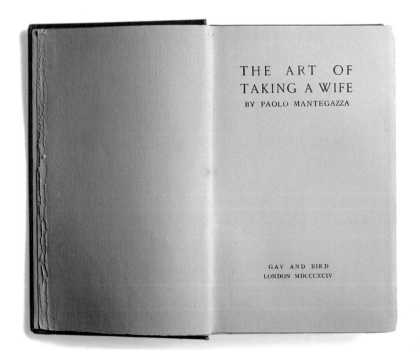

THE ART OF
TAKING A WIFE
BY PAOLO MANTEGAZZA

GAY AND BIRD
LONDON MDCCCXCIV